JAN 2018.

To Simon:

Happy Birthday!
Have a spicy time!!
Love Pat B Rosy.
xxx.

CHILLI
COOKBOOK

Editor:
Valerie Ferguson

LORENZ BOOKS

Contents

Introduction   4

Types of Chillies   6

Chilli Products   7

Techniques   8

Spicy Soups, Dips & Appetizers   10

Fiery Fish & Shellfish   22

Sizzling Chicken & Meat Dishes   32

Hot Vegetarian Dishes   46

Piquant Side Dishes & Salads   58

Index   64

Introduction

Chilli peppers, in their many and varied forms, fresh and dried, are widely used in cooking throughout the world. Native to Central and South America, they were "discovered" in the 16th century by the Spanish *conquistadores,* who brought them back to Europe, from where they spread to the East.

Chillies are known for their heat, but can also be quite subtle, bringing extra depth of flavour to dishes such as casseroles without making them at all fiery if you select and use them with care. Remember that the smallest chillies tend to be the hottest, and if you wish to reduce the heat of any variety you can simply remove its seeds and, of course, use less of it. Chilli products such as cayenne pepper and Tabasco sauce are extremely useful in the kitchen as only very small amounts can add a real zing to food.

Chillies combine well with all kinds of fish and shellfish, poultry, meat, vegetables, salads, grains and pulses. As well as being pleasurable to eat, they aid the digestion, are a useful source of vitamins A and C, and are said to have a beneficial calming effect – all of which seem excellent reasons to cook with them more often!

Types of Chillies

The following are just a few of the many different kinds of chillies.

Ancho
These are dried poblano chillies. They are mild and quite sweet.

Bird's Eye
These chillies are so hot that they taste explosive to the uninitiated. They can be green, red or orange in colour.

Cascabel
Round, dried cascabel chillies rattle when they are shaken.

Chipotle
These dried, smoked jalapeño chillies, give an intense heat to stews.

Guajillo
Fairly mild in flavour, and very good with most seafood.

Habanero
Also known as Scotch Bonnets, these chillies are extremely hot. They are used in Caribbean jerk sauces.

Below: Thai chillies.

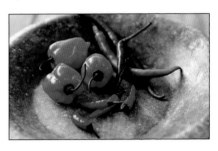

Above: Clockwise from top left; Habanero, Indian, and bird's eye chillies.

Indian
Small and very hot, these are widely used in curry dishes.

Jalapeño
Available fresh or bottled, jalapeños are used in Mexican salsas and sauces.

Nyora
A dried, lightly-smoked Spanish chilli with a sweet, fruity flavour.

Poblano
These large, mild chillies ripen to a dark red, and are used for stuffing, in the Mexican dish Chillies Rellenos.

Serrano
Small chillies with a biting flavour often used raw in salsas.

Thai
These tiny chillies are fairly hot and are used in green Thai curry pastes.

Chilli Products

A range of flavouring ingredients are based on chillies.

Chilli Powder
Milder than cayenne and more coarsely ground, this is prepared from a variety of mild to hot chillies. Some brands also contain other flavourings, such as cumin and oregano – added for convenience in the preparation of dishes such as chilli con carne.

Above: Ground chilli.

Dried Chilli Flakes
These contain both the flesh and seeds of red chillies and can be used whole to pep up cooked dishes.

Chilli Oil
This is excellent for flavouring food during frying, or for basting meat or fish for barbecuing.

Chilli Paste
Ready-made chilli paste is sold in small jars. It is also easy to prepare at home from fresh chillies with a food processor. It can be stored in the fridge for 1 week or frozen in small batches.

Chilli Sauce
The best-known chilli sauce is probably Tabasco, which is made from extremely hot chillies mixed with salt and vinegar, then matured for several years. There is a growing variety of other brands however, with many different blends and characteristics. Chilli sauce is widely used at the table in small quantities for seasoning dishes.

Sweet Chilli Sauce
A popular condiment in Thai, Malaysian, and Western cuisine, this sweet, tangy sauce is made from mild red chillies. It is often used as a dip for fried food.

Cayenne Pepper
This finely ground powder, made from a variety of red chilli, comes in hot, sweet or smoked varities. The hot type is extremely fiery and is used in tiny amounts as a seasoning, for example in egg and cheese dishes.

CHOOSING CHILLIES
• Fresh chillies should be firm, glossy and evenly coloured. Avoid musty, soft or wrinkled chillies.
• Dried chilli flakes and ground chillies should have a good aroma and colour. Buy them in small quantities and date the packaging so that you do not keep them too long.

Techniques

Removing Seeds from Fresh Chillies

1 Using a sharp knife, hold the chilli firmly at the stalk end and cut it in half lengthways. Remove the stalk from the chilli, also removing a thin slice from the top.

2 Using a small, sharp knife, scrape out the seeds and fleshy white ribs from each half.

TREATING "BURNS"

If you have managed to get chilli oil on delicate skin, an alkali such as a paste made from bicarbonate of soda mixed with cold water will ease the discomfort.

Roasting & Peeling Fresh Chillies

1 Dry-fry the chillies in a frying pan until the skin is scorched all over. Alternatively, spear them on a long-handled metal skewer and place them over the flame of a gas burner to roast until the skin blisters and darkens. Be careful not to let the flesh burn.

2 Place the roasted chillies in a strong plastic bag while they are still hot and tie the top to keep the steam in. Set aside for 20 minutes, then peel off the blistered skin.

3 Cut off the stalks, slit the chillies lengthways and scrape out the seeds with a small, sharp knife.

Soaking Dried Chillies

To bring out the flavour of dried chillies, it is best to soak them for up to 1 hour before use.

1 Soak the chillies in hot water for about 10 minutes (longer if possible) until the colour is restored and the chilli has swelled and softened. Drain.

2 Cut off the stalks, then slit the chillies lengthways and scrape out the seeds. Slice or chop the flesh. For puréed chillies, put in a food processor or blender with a little soaking water and process until smooth.

STORING CHILLIES
• Store fresh chillies in a plastic bag in the chiller compartment of the fridge for a week or more.
• Fresh chillies can also be frozen. There is no need to blanch them if you plan to use them fairly quickly.
• Store dried and ground chillies in airtight jars in a cool place out of direct sunlight.
• To dry chillies, thread on a string, hang in a warm, dry place until crumbly, then crush in a mortar.

Grinding Dried Chillies

This method gives a distinctive and smoky taste to the resulting chilli powder and is worth the effort.

1 Soak the dried chillies in water, then drain and pat dry with kitchen paper. Dry-fry in a heavy-based pan until crisp.

2 Transfer to a mortar and grind to a fine powder with a pestle. Store in an airtight container.

COOKING TIPS
• To bring out the flavour of chillies, dry-roast them in a hot non-stick frying pan for a few minutes. Do not allow them to change colour.
• To reduce the heat of fresh or dried chillies, soak them for an hour in a solution of wine vinegar and salt in the ratio 3:1.
• If you bite into a chilli that is uncomfortably hot, swallow a spoonful of sugar. Don't be tempted to gulp down a glass of water or beer; this will only succeed in spreading the heat further.

Corn & Sweet Potato Soup with Chilli

Chilli injects an appealing zing into this otherwise mild and sweet vegetable combination, which makes a colourful and unusual first course for an informal dinner party or a light lunch dish.

Serves 6

INGREDIENTS
15 ml/1 tbsp olive oil
1 onion, finely chopped
2 garlic cloves, crushed
1 small red chilli, seeded and
    finely chopped
1.75 litres/3 pints/7½ cups vegetable stock
10 ml/2 tsp ground cumin
1 medium sweet potato, diced
½ red (bell) pepper, finely chopped
450 g/1 lb sweetcorn kernels
salt and freshly ground
    black pepper
fresh parsley, chopped, to serve

1 Heat the oil in a large, heavy-based pan. Add the chopped onion and fry for 5 minutes until softened. Add the crushed garlic and finely chopped red chilli and continue to fry for a further 2 minutes.

2 Pour in 300 ml/½ pint/1¼ cups of the stock and simmer for 10 minutes. Mix the cumin with a little stock to form a paste and stir into the soup.

3 Add the diced sweet potato, stir and bring to the boil. Lower the heat and simmer, covered, for 10 minutes. Season with salt and freshly ground black pepper and stir again.

4 Add the red pepper, sweetcorn and remaining stock and simmer for a further 10 minutes. Pour half of the soup into a food processor or blender and process until smooth then stir back into the pan. Serve in warmed bowls garnished with chopped parsley.

VARIATION: Yellow or orange (bell) peppers can be used instead of red, but green are too bitter.

Spicy Chicken Soup

An aromatic soup with coconut, galangal, lemon grass and chilli.

Serves 4–6

INGREDIENTS
750 ml/1¼ pints/3 cups coconut milk
475 ml/16 fl oz/2 cups chicken stock
4 lemon grass stalks, bruised and chopped
1 red chilli, seeded and finely chopped
2.5 cm/1 in piece galangal, thinly sliced
10 black peppercorns, crushed
10 fresh kaffir lime leaves, torn
300 g/11 oz chicken, cut into thin strips
115 g/4 oz button mushrooms
50 g/2 oz baby sweetcorn
60 ml/4 tbsp lime juice
45 ml/3 tbsp Thai fish sauce
chopped red chilli, spring onions (scallions) and fresh coriander (cilantro), to garnish

1 Bring the coconut milk and stock to the boil. Add the lemon grass, chilli, galangal, peppercorns and half the lime leaves. Lower the heat and simmer gently for 10 minutes.

2 Strain into a clean pan. Return to the heat, add the chicken, mushrooms and sweetcorn and simmer for 5–7 minutes to cook the chicken.

3 Stir in the lime juice, fish sauce to taste and the remaining lime leaves. Serve in warmed bowls, garnished with chopped chilli, spring onions and coriander.

Hot & Sour Soup

A classic Thai seafood soup with a generous helping of chillies.

Serves 4–6

INGREDIENTS
450 g/1 lb raw king prawns (jumbo shrimp) in the shell
1 litre/1¾ pints/4 cups chicken stock or water
3 lemon grass stalks, bruised
10 fresh kaffir lime leaves, torn in half
225 g/8 oz can straw mushrooms, drained
45 ml/3 tbsp Thai fish sauce
50 ml/2 fl oz/¼ cup lime juice
15 ml/1 tbsp fresh coriander (cilantro) leaves
4 red chillies, seeded and chopped
2 spring onions (scallions), finely chopped

1 Peel and devein the prawns and set aside. Place the shells in a pan with the stock or water and bring to the boil. Add the lemon grass stalks and half the lime leaves. Simmer for 5–6 minutes until the stock is fragrant.

2 Strain, return to the pan and reheat. Add the mushrooms and prawns, then cook until the prawns turn pink.

3 Stir in the remaining ingredients. Taste and adjust the seasoning: it should be sour, salty, spicy and hot. Serve the soup in warmed bowls.

*Right: Spicy Chicken Soup (top);
Hot & Sour Soup*

Chilli, Tomato & Basil Dip

A versatile, spicy dip, delicious served with all kinds of savoury dishes.

Serves 4

INGREDIENTS
1 shallot
2 garlic cloves
1 handful fresh basil leaves, plus extra
   to garnish
500 g/1¼ lb ripe tomatoes
30 ml/2 tbsp olive oil
2 green chillies
salt and freshly ground black pepper

1 Peel and halve the shallot and garlic cloves. Place in a food processor or blender with the basil leaves and process until very finely chopped.

2 Halve the tomatoes and add to the shallot mixture. Pulse until well blended and finely chopped. With the motor still running, slowly pour in the olive oil. Season to taste.

3 Halve the chillies lengthways and discard the seeds. Finely slice the flesh into tiny strips and stir into the dip. Serve at room temperature, garnished with a few torn basil leaves.

COOK'S TIP: This dip is best made with full-flavoured sun-ripened tomatoes. In winter, use a drained 400 g/14 oz can of plum tomatoes.

Avocado, Chilli & Red Onion Salsa

This simple, crunchy salsa is a refreshing fire-and-ice mixture.

Serves 4

INGREDIENTS

2 ripe avocados,
  halved and stoned
1 red onion, finely chopped
1 red (bell) pepper
4 green chillies
30 ml/2 tbsp chopped fresh coriander
  (cilantro)
30 ml/2 tbsp sunflower oil
juice of 1 lemon
salt and freshly ground black pepper
tortilla chips, to serve

1 Cut out the flesh of the avocado, and finely dice. Slice the top off the pepper and pull out the central core. Shake out any remaining seeds. Cut the pepper into thin strips and then into dice. Halve the chillies, discard the seeds and finely chop the flesh.

2 In a large bowl mix the chillies, coriander, oil and lemon juice, add salt and pepper to taste.

3 Add the prepared avocado, red onion and pepper to the bowl. Toss to mix, and serve with tortilla chips.

Piri-piri Prawns with Aïoli

Piri-piri is a Portuguese hot pepper sauce. The name means "small chilli".

Serves 4

INGREDIENTS
1 red chilli, seeded and finely chopped,
   plus extra whole chillies to garnish
2.5 ml/½ tsp paprika
2.5 ml/½ tsp ground coriander
1 garlic clove, crushed
juice of ½ lime
30 ml/2 tbsp olive oil
20 large raw prawns (shrimp) in the shell,
   heads removed and deveined
salt and freshly ground black pepper

FOR THE AÏOLI
150 ml/¼ pint/⅔ cup mayonnaise
2 garlic cloves, crushed
5 ml/1 tsp Dijon mustard

1 To make the aïoli, mix the mayonnaise, garlic and mustard in a small bowl and set aside.

2 Mix the chopped chilli, paprika, coriander, garlic, lime juice and olive oil in a bowl. Season to taste with salt and freshly ground black pepper. Add the prepared prawns and mix well. Cover and leave to marinate in a cool place for 30 minutes.

3 Thread the prawns on to skewers and grill or barbecue, basting and turning the skewers frequently, for 6–8 minutes, or until the prawns are pink. Serve with the aïoli, garnished with whole chillies.

Mussels with a Chilli Sauce

Superb, spiced seafood – East meets West in the fiery coconut sauce.

Serves 4

INGREDIENTS
1.3 kg/3 lb fresh mussels, cleaned
45 ml/3 tbsp dry sherry
45 ml/3 tbsp fish stock
400 ml/14 fl oz/1⅔ cups coconut milk
150 ml/¼ pint/⅔ cup water
30 ml/2 tbsp olive oil
1 onion, chopped
2 garlic cloves, crushed
1 lemon grass stalk, sliced
30 ml/2 tbsp tomato purée (paste)
10 ml/2 tsp Thai red curry paste
15 ml/1 tbsp grated fresh root ginger
1 red chilli, seeded and sliced
15 ml/1 tbsp cornflour (cornstarch)
60 ml/4 tbsp chopped coriander (cilantro)
salt and freshly ground black pepper
French bread, to serve

1 Discard any open mussels that do not close when tapped. Place the rest in a large pan with the sherry, stock, coconut milk and water. Bring to the boil, cover and cook for 5 minutes. Strain the juices into a bowl. Return the mussels to the pan, discarding any that stay closed. Cover to keep warm.

2 Heat the oil in another pan and fry the onion and garlic for 5 minutes to soften. Add the lemon grass, tomato purée, curry paste, ginger, chilli and retained cooking juices. Season with pepper and simmer for 5 minutes.

3 Blend the cornflour to a thin paste and stir into the pan. Bring to the boil, stirring. Stir in the mussels, sprinkle with coriander and serve.

Spicy Potato Wedges with Chilli Dip

For a healthy snack or accompaniment with superb flavour, try these roasted potato wedges. The chilli dip complements them perfectly.

Serves 2

INGREDIENTS
2 baking potatoes, about 225 g/8 oz each
30 ml/2 tbsp olive oil
2 garlic cloves, crushed
5 ml/1 tsp ground allspice
5 ml/1 tsp ground coriander
15 ml/1 tbsp paprika
salt and freshly ground black pepper

FOR THE CHILLI DIP
15 ml/1 tbsp olive oil
1 small onion, finely chopped
1 garlic clove, crushed
200 g/7 oz canned chopped tomatoes
1 red chilli, seeded and finely chopped
15 ml/1 tbsp balsamic vinegar
15 ml/1 tbsp chopped fresh coriander
   (cilantro), plus whole sprigs to garnish

1 Preheat the oven to 200°C/400°F/ Gas 6. Cut the potatoes in half, then into eight wedges.

COOK'S TIP: If you wish, these potatoes can be partly prepared in advance. Parboil the wedges until softened, and add to the tin as instructed in step 3. Store in the refrigerator and roast when ready.

2 Place the wedges in a pan of cold water. Bring to the boil, then lower the heat and simmer gently for 10 minutes or until the potatoes have softened slightly. Drain well and pat dry on kitchen paper.

3 Mix the oil, garlic, ground allspice, coriander and paprika in a roasting tin. Add salt and pepper to taste. Add the potato wedges to the tin and shake to coat them thoroughly. Roast for 20 minutes, turning occasionally, until the potato wedges are browned, crisp and fully cooked.

4 Meanwhile, to make the chilli dip, heat the oil in a pan, add the onion and garlic and cook them for 5–10 minutes until soft. Add the tomatoes with their juice. Stir in the chilli and vinegar. Cook gently for 10 minutes until the mixture has reduced and thickened slightly.

5 Taste and adjust the seasoning as necessary. Stir in the chopped coriander and pour the dip into a warmed bowl.

6 Serve the dip hot with the roasted potato wedges, garnished with whole coriander sprigs.

Chilli Onion Koftas

These delicious Indian onion fritters are made with chickpea flour, fresh green chillies and spices. They are served with a cooling yogurt dip.

Serves 4–5

INGREDIENTS
675 g/1½ lb onions, halved and
    thinly sliced
5 ml/1 tsp salt
5 ml/1 tsp ground coriander
5 ml/1 tsp ground cumin
2.5 ml/½ tsp ground turmeric
1–2 green chillies, seeded and finely
    chopped
45 ml/3 tbsp chopped fresh coriander
    (cilantro)
90 g/3¼ oz/¾ cup chickpea (gram) flour
2.5 ml/½ tsp baking powder
vegetable oil, for deep-frying

TO SERVE
lemon wedges
fresh coriander (cilantro) sprigs
yogurt and herb dip or yogurt and
    cucumber dip (see Cook's Tips)

1 Place the sliced onions in a colander, add the salt and toss well. Place them on a plate and leave to stand for about 45 minutes, tossing them once or twice with a fork. Rinse the onions, then squeeze out excess moisture from them.

2 Place the onions in a bowl. Add the ground coriander, cumin, turmeric, chopped chillies and fresh coriander. Mix well.

3 Add the chickpea flour and baking powder, then use your hands to mix all the ingredients thoroughly. Shape the mixture into 12–15 koftas, about the size of golf balls.

4 Heat the oil for deep-frying to 180–190°C/350–375°F or until a cube of day-old bread browns in 30–45 seconds. Fry the koftas, four or five at a time, until they are deep golden brown all over.

5 Drain each batch on kitchen paper and keep warm until they are all cooked. Serve with lemon wedges, coriander sprigs and a yogurt dip.

COOK'S TIPS:

• To make a yogurt and herb dip, stir 30 ml/2 tbsp each chopped fresh coriander (cilantro) and mint into about 250 ml/8 fl oz/1 cup plain yogurt. Season with salt, toasted cumin seeds and muscovado sugar.

• For a cucumber dip, stir half a diced cucumber and one seeded and chopped green chilli into 250 ml/ 8 fl oz/1 cup set plain yogurt. Season the mixture to taste with salt and ground cumin.

Steamed Fish with Red Chilli Sauce

Steaming a whole fish like this retains all the flavour and keeps it moist. The accompanying sauce packs a real punch.

Serves 4

INGREDIENTS
1 large or 2 medium firm fish, such as sea bass or grouper, scaled and cleaned
1 fresh banana leaf
30 ml/2 tbsp rice wine
3 red chillies, seeded and finely sliced
2 garlic cloves, finely chopped
2 cm/¾ in piece fresh root ginger, peeled and finely shredded
2 lemon grass stalks, crushed and finely chopped
2 spring onions (scallions), chopped
30 ml/2 tbsp Thai fish sauce
juice of 1 lime

FOR THE CHILLI SAUCE
10 red chillies, seeded and chopped
4 garlic cloves, chopped
60 ml/4 tbsp Thai fish sauce
15 ml/1 tbsp sugar
75 ml/5 tbsp lime juice

1 Rinse the fish under cold running water. Pat dry with kitchen paper. With a sharp knife, slash the skin of the fish a few times on both sides.

COOK'S TIP: Banana leaves can be bought in Asian stores. If unavailable, use kitchen foil.

2 Place the fish on a banana leaf. Mix together all the remaining ingredients and spread over the fish.

3 Place a rack or small upturned plate in the bottom of a wok and then add 5 cm/2 in boiling water; place a banana leaf on top. Lift the banana leaf holding the fish and place on the rack or plate. Cover with a lid and steam for about 10–15 minutes or until the fish is cooked.

4 To make the chilli sauce, place all the ingredients in a food processor and process until smooth. You may need to add a little cold water if the sauce seems too thick.

5 Transfer the chilli sauce to a small serving bowl. Serve the fish hot, on the banana leaf if liked, accompanied by the sauce to spoon over the top.

Red Snapper with Chilli, Gin & Ginger Sauce

Fresh chillies, ginger and gin add piquancy to a fine fish dish that tastes every bit as good as it looks.

Serves 4

INGREDIENTS
1.3 kg/3 lb red snapper, scaled and cleaned
30 ml/2 tbsp sunflower oil
1 onion, chopped
2 garlic cloves, crushed
50 g/2 oz/¾ cup sliced button (white)
    mushrooms
5 ml/1 tsp ground coriander
15 ml/1 tbsp chopped fresh parsley
30 ml/2 tbsp grated fresh root ginger
2 red chillies, seeded and sliced
15 ml/1 tbsp cornflour (cornstarch)
45 ml/3 tbsp gin
300 ml/½ pint/1¼ cups chicken or vegetable
    stock
salt and freshly ground black pepper

FOR THE GARNISH
15 ml/1 tbsp sunflower oil
6 garlic cloves, sliced
1 lettuce heart, finely shredded
1 bunch fresh coriander (cilantro), tied with
    red raffia

1 Preheat the oven to 190°C/375°F/
Gas 5. Grease a flameproof dish large
enough to hold the fish. Make several
diagonal cuts on one side of the fish.

2 Heat the oil in a frying pan and fry
the onion, garlic and mushrooms for
2–3 minutes. Stir in the ground
coriander and chopped parsley. Season
with salt and pepper.

3 Spoon the vegetable mixture into
the fish cavity, then lift the snapper
into the dish. Pour in enough cold
water to cover the bottom of the dish.
Sprinkle the ginger and chillies over,
then cover and bake the fish for
30–40 minutes, basting from time
to time. Remove the cover for the
last 10 minutes.

4 Carefully lift the snapper on to a serving dish and keep hot. Tip the cooking juices into a pan.

5 Blend together the cornflour and gin and stir into the cooking juices. Pour in the stock. Bring to the boil and cook gently for 3–4 minutes or until thickened, stirring all the time. Adjust the seasoning to taste, then pour into a sauce-boat.

6 To make the garnish, heat the oil in a frying pan and stir-fry the sliced garlic and shredded lettuce over a high heat until crisp. Spoon alongside the snapper. Place the coriander bouquet on the other side. Serve with the sauce.

VARIATION: If red snapper is not available, try using red or grey mullet instead.

Indian-spiced Fish Stew

A fiery dish made with potatoes, tomatoes and traditional Indian spices.

Serves 4

INGREDIENTS
30 ml/2 tbsp oil
5 ml/1 tsp cumin seeds
1 onion, chopped
1 red (bell) pepper, seeded and thinly sliced
1 garlic clove, crushed
2 red chillies, seeded and finely chopped
2 bay leaves
2.5 ml/½ tsp salt
5 ml/1 tsp ground cumin
5 ml/1 tsp ground coriander
5 ml/1 tsp chilli powder
400 g/14 oz can chopped tomatoes
2 large potatoes, cut into 2.5 cm/1 in chunks
300 ml/½ pint/1¼ cups fish stock
4 cod fillets
chappatis, to serve

1 Heat the oil in a large, deep-sided frying pan and fry the cumin seeds for 2 minutes until they begin to splutter. Add the onion, red pepper, garlic, chopped chillies and bay leaves and fry the mixture for 5–7 minutes until the onions have browned.

2 Add the salt, ground cumin, ground coriander and chilli powder and cook for 3–4 minutes. Stir in the tomatoes, potatoes and fish stock. Bring to the boil and then allow to simmer for a further 10 minutes.

3 Add the fish, then cover and leave to simmer for 10 more minutes or until the fish is tender. Serve the stew with chappatis.

Chilli Crabs

A spicy paste forms the basis of the sauce for this finger-licking dish.

Serves 4

INGREDIENTS

2 cooked crabs, about 675 g/1½ lb total
    weight
1 cm/½ in cube prepared *terasi* (fermented
    shrimp paste)
2 garlic cloves
2 red chillies, seeded, or 5 ml/1 tsp chopped
    chilli from a jar
1 cm/½ in piece fresh root ginger, peeled
    and sliced
60 ml/4 tbsp sunflower oil
300 ml/½ pint/1¼ cups tomato ketchup
15 ml/1 tbsp dark soft brown sugar
150 ml/¼ pint/⅔ cup warm water
4 spring onions (scallions), chopped,
    cucumber chunks and hot toast, to serve
    (optional)

1 For each crab, remove the large claws and turn on to its back, with the head facing away. Use your thumbs to push the body up from the main shell. Discard the stomach sac and "dead men's fingers". Leave the creamy brown meat in the shell and cut the shell in half. Cut the body section in half and crack the claws without splintering.

2 Grind the *terasi,* garlic, chillies and ginger to a paste in a food processor or with a pestle and mortar. Heat a wok and add the oil. Fry the paste, stirring it all the time, without browning. Stir in the ketchup, sugar and water. When just boiling, add all the crab and toss until hot. Toss in the chopped spring onions and serve with cucumber and toast, if liked.

Caribbean Chilli-spiced Fish Cakes with Tomato Dip

The flavour of white fish and crab meat is set off perfectly by hot chilli, which is also used in the accompanying tomato dip.

Makes about 15

INGREDIENTS
115 g/4 oz skinless white fish fillet, cooked
115 g/4 oz white crab meat (fresh, frozen or canned)
115 g/4 oz cooked floury potatoes, mashed
30 ml/2 tbsp fresh herb seasoning
2.5 ml/½ tsp mild mustard
2.5 ml/½ tsp freshly ground black pepper
½ hot chilli, seeded and finely chopped
10 ml/2 tsp fresh oregano
1 egg, beaten
plain (all-purpose) flour, for dredging
vegetable oil, for frying
lime wedges, fresh coriander (cilantro) sprigs and whole chillies, to garnish

FOR THE TOMATO DIP
15 g/½ oz/1 tbsp butter
½ onion, finely chopped
2 canned plum tomatoes, chopped
1 garlic clove, crushed
150 ml/¼ pint/⅔ cup water
5–10 ml/1–2 tsp malt vinegar
15 ml/1 tbsp chopped fresh coriander (cilantro)
½ hot chilli, seeded and chopped

1 Flake the cooked fish into a large bowl. Mix in the crab meat, mashed potatoes, mustard, freshly ground black pepper, chilli and oregano

2 Add the beaten egg to the fish mixture and combine well. Chill in the refrigerator for at least 30 minutes.

3 To make the tomato dip, melt the butter in a small pan over a medium heat. Add the onion, tomatoes and garlic and sauté for about 5 minutes until the onion is tender.

4 Add the water, vinegar, coriander and chilli to the pan. Bring to the boil, then reduce the heat and allow to simmer for 10 minutes.

5 Transfer the mixture to a food processor or blender and pulse to a smooth purée. Transfer the dip into a bowl. Keep warm or chill as preferred.

6 Using a spoon, shape the fish mixture into rounds.

7 Dredge the fish balls with flour, shaking off the excess. Heat a little oil in a frying pan and fry, a few at a time, for 2–3 minutes on each side. Drain on kitchen paper and keep warm while cooking the remainder.

8 Serve the fish cakes hot with the tomato dip and garnished with lime wedges, fresh coriander sprigs and whole chillies.

Marinated Squid Risotto with Chilli

Here squid is cooked very quickly after being steeped in a tenderizing chilli marinade. It is then added to a spicy risotto.

Serves 3–4

INGREDIENTS
about 450 g/1 lb squid, cleaned and cut
   into thin strips
about 45 ml/3 tbsp olive oil
15 g/½ oz/1 tbsp butter
1 onion, finely chopped
2 garlic cloves, crushed
1 red chilli, seeded and finely sliced
275 g/10 oz/1½ cups risotto rice
175 ml/6 fl oz/¾ cup dry white wine
1 litre/1¾ pints/4 cups simmering fish stock
30 ml/2 tbsp chopped fresh coriander
   (cilantro)
salt and freshly ground black pepper

FOR THE MARINADE
2 ripe kiwi fruit, chopped and mashed
1 red chilli, seeded and finely sliced
30 ml/2 tbsp lime juice

1 To make the marinade, place the mashed kiwi in a bowl with the chilli and lime juice. Add the squid strips, season and stir to coat well. Cover and set aside in the fridge for 4 hours.

COOK'S TIP: Although fish stock underlines the flavour of the squid, a light chicken or vegetable stock would also work well in this recipe.

2 Drain the squid. Heat 15 ml/1 tbsp of the oil in a large frying pan and cook the squid, in batches if necessary, for 30–60 seconds over a high heat. It is important that the squid cooks very quickly.

3 Transfer the cooked squid to a plate and set aside. As you cook, pour the juices into a jug and reserve, adding more oil to the pan as necessary.

4 Heat the remaining oil with the butter in a large pan and gently fry the onion and garlic for about 5–6 minutes until soft. Add the chilli and fry for 1 minute more.

5 Add the risotto rice. Cook for a few minutes, stirring, until the rice is coated with oil and has become slightly translucent. Add the wine and stir the rice until all the liquid has been absorbed.

6 Gradually add the hot stock and the reserved cooking liquid from the squid, a ladleful at a time, stirring constantly and allowing each quantity of stock to be absorbed before adding the next.

7 When the rice is about three-quarters cooked, stir in the squid and continue cooking until all the stock has been absorbed and the rice is tender, but retains a bit of "bite". Stir in the coriander, cover with a lid or dish towel and leave to rest for a few minutes before serving.

Chicken with Chipotle Sauce

It is important to seek out chipotle chillies for this recipe, as they impart a wonderfully rich and smoky flavour to the chicken breasts.

Serves 6

INGREDIENTS
6 chipotle chillies
200 ml/7 fl oz/scant 1 cup hot water
chicken stock (see method for quantity)
45 ml/3 tbsp vegetable oil
3 onions, thinly sliced
6 skinless boneless chicken breast fillets
salt and freshly ground black pepper
fresh oregano, to garnish
boiled white rice and beans, to serve

1 Put the dried chillies in a bowl and cover with hot water. Leave to stand for about 30 minutes until very soft. Drain, reserving the soaking water in a measuring jug.

2 Cut off the stalk of each chilli, then slit them in half lengthways and scrape out the seeds with a small, sharp knife.

3 Preheat the oven to 180°C/350°F/Gas 4. Chop the flesh of the chillies roughly and put it in a food processor or blender. Add enough chicken stock to the soaking water to make it up to 400 ml/14 fl oz/1⅔ cups. Pour it into the processor or blender and process at maximum power until smooth.

4 Heat the oil in a large frying pan. Add the onions and cook over a moderate heat for about 5 minutes, stirring occasionally, until softened but not coloured.

5 Using a slotted spoon, transfer the onion slices to a casserole large enough to hold all the chicken breasts in a single layer. Arrange the chicken breasts on top and season with salt and freshly ground black pepper.

COOK'S TIP: If you are a lover of chipotle chillies, you may wish to use more than six.

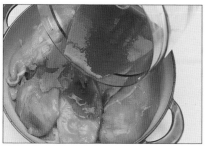

6 Pour the chipotle purée over the chicken breasts, making sure that each piece is evenly coated.

7 Cook in the oven for 45 minutes– 1 hour or until the chicken is cooked through, but is still moist and tender. Garnish with fresh oregano and serve with boiled white rice and beans.

Barbecued Jerk Chicken

Jerk seasoning is from Jamaica, and is often used with chicken and pork.

Serves 4

INGREDIENTS
8 chicken thigh and drumstick portions
oil, for brushing
salad leaves, to serve

FOR THE JERK SEASONING
5 ml/1 tsp ground allspice
5 ml/1 tsp ground cinnamon
5 ml/1 tsp dried thyme
1.5 ml/¼ tsp grated nutmeg
10 ml/2 tsp demerara sugar
2 garlic cloves, crushed
15 ml/1 tbsp finely chopped onion
15 ml/1 tbsp sliced spring onions (scallions)
15 ml/1 tbsp vinegar
30 ml/2 tbsp oil
15 ml/1 tbsp lime juice
1 hot chilli, chopped
salt and black pepper

1 To make the marinade, combine all the ingredients in a small bowl. Using a fork, mash them together well to form a thick paste.

2 Lay the chicken pieces on a plate or board and make several lengthways slits in the flesh. Rub the seasoning all over the chicken and into the slits.

3 Place the chicken pieces in a dish, cover with clear film and marinate overnight in the fridge.

4 Shake off any excess seasoning from the chicken. Brush with oil and place either on a baking sheet or on a barbecue grill. Cook under a preheated grill for 45 minutes, turning often, or barbecue over hot coals for 30 minutes. Serve hot with salad leaves.

Hot Chilli Chicken

This fiery-hot curry has a wonderful depth of flavour.

Serves 4

INGREDIENTS

2 green and 5 dried red chillies
30 ml/2 tbsp tomato purée (paste)
2 garlic cloves, roughly chopped
2.5 ml/½ tsp salt
1.5 ml/¼ tsp sugar
5 ml/1 tsp chilli powder
2.5 ml/½ tsp paprika
15 ml/1 tbsp curry paste
30 ml/2 tbsp oil
2.5 ml/½ tsp cumin seeds
1 onion, finely chopped
2 bay leaves
5 ml/1 tsp ground coriander
5 ml/1 tsp ground cumin
1.5 ml/¼ tsp ground turmeric
400 g/14 oz can chopped tomatoes
8 chicken thighs, skinned and boned
5 ml/1 tsp garam masala

1 Roughly chop all the chillies. Put in a food processor or blender with the tomato purée, garlic, salt, sugar, chilli powder, paprika and curry paste and process to a smooth paste.

2 Heat the oil in a large pan and fry the cumin seeds for 2 minutes. Add the onion and bay leaves and fry for about 5 minutes. Add the chilli paste and fry for 2–3 minutes. Add the remaining ground spices and cook for 2 minutes. Add the chopped tomatoes and 150 ml/¼ pint/⅔ cup water. Bring to the boil and simmer for 5 minutes until the sauce thickens.

3 Add the chicken and garam masala. Cover and simmer for 25–30 minutes until tender. Chappatis and yogurt with sliced chillies go well with this.

Penne with Tomato & Chilli Sauce

This famous pasta dish is known in Italy as *penne all'arrabbiata* — *arrabbiata* (literally "furious") referring to the fiery nature of the chilli.

Serves 4

INGREDIENTS
25 g/1 oz dried porcini mushrooms
90 g/3½ oz/7 tbsp butter
150 g/5 oz pancetta lardons or rindless
   smoked streaky (fatty) bacon, diced
1–2 dried red chillies, to taste
2 garlic cloves, crushed
8 ripe Italian plum tomatoes, peeled
   and chopped
a few fresh basil leaves, torn, plus extra
   to garnish
350 g/12 oz/3 cups dried penne
50 g/2 oz/⅔ cup grated Parmesan cheese
25 g/1 oz/⅓ cup grated Pecorino cheese

1 Soak the dried mushrooms in warm water to cover for 15–20 minutes. Drain, then squeeze dry with your hands. Finely chop the mushrooms.

2 Melt 50 g/2 oz/¼ cup of the butter in a medium frying pan or pan. Add the pancetta or bacon and stir-fry over a medium heat until golden and slightly crispy. Remove with a slotted spoon and set aside.

3 Add the chopped mushrooms to the pan and cook in the same way. Remove and set aside with the pancetta or bacon.

4 Crumble in one chilli, add the garlic and cook, stirring, for a few minutes until the garlic turns golden.

5 Add the tomatoes and basil and season with salt. Cook gently, stirring occasionally, for 10–15 minutes. Meanwhile, cook the penne in a pan of boiling salted water until *al dente*.

6 Add the pancetta or bacon and the mushrooms to the tomato sauce. Taste for seasoning, adding more chillies if you like. If the sauce is too dry, stir in a little of the pasta water.

7 Drain the pasta and tip it into a warmed bowl. Dice the remaining butter, add it to the pasta with the cheeses, then toss until well coated. Pour the tomato sauce over the pasta, toss well and serve immediately, with a few basil leaves sprinkled on top.

VARIATIONS: There are many different versions of this dish. It is sometimes made without the meat, and fresh parsley is occasionally used instead of the basil used here.

Spicy Lamb & Potato Curry

Transform these simple ingredients into a tasty curry with the addition of Indian spices and fresh green chilli.

Serves 4

INGREDIENTS
45 ml/3 tbsp oil
1 onion, finely chopped
2 bay leaves
1 green chilli, seeded and finely chopped
2 garlic cloves, finely chopped
675 g/1½ lb lamb fillet
10 ml/2 tsp ground coriander
5 ml/1 tsp ground cumin
2.5 ml/½ tsp ground turmeric
2.5 ml/½ tsp chilli powder
2.5 ml/½ tsp salt
225 g/8 oz tomatoes, skinned and finely chopped
600 ml/1 pint/2½ cups lamb stock
2 large potatoes, cut into 2.5 cm/1 in chunks
chopped fresh coriander (cilantro), to garnish
chappatis, to serve (optional)

1 Heat the oil in a large pan and fry the onion, bay leaves, chilli and garlic over medium heat for 5 minutes.

2 Remove any visible fat from the lamb. Cut the meat into 2.5 cm/1 in cubes. Add to the pan and cook for 6–8 minutes until lightly browned.

3 Add the ground coriander, cumin, turmeric, chilli powder and salt and cook for 3–4 minutes, stirring the mixture all the time to prevent the spices from sticking to the bottom of the pan.

4 Add the chopped tomatoes and lamb stock and simmer for 5 minutes until the sauce thickens. Bring to the boil, then cover, reduce the heat to very low and simmer for 1 hour.

5 Add the potatoes to the curry and continue to cook for a further 30–40 minutes or until the meat is tender. Garnish the curry with the chopped fresh coriander and serve with chappatis, if you like.

Tex-mex Baked Potatoes with Chilli

Classic chilli beef tops crisp, floury-centred baked potatoes. Easy to prepare and great for a simple yet substantial family supper.

Serves 4

INGREDIENTS
4 medium baking potatoes
15 ml/1 tbsp vegetable oil, plus extra
    for brushing
1 garlic clove, crushed
1 small onion, chopped
½ red (bell) pepper, seeded and chopped
225 g/8 oz lean minced (ground) beef
½ small red chilli, seeded and chopped
5 ml/1 tsp ground cumin
pinch of cayenne pepper
200 g/7 oz can chopped tomatoes
30 ml/2 tbsp tomato purée (paste)
2.5 ml/½ tsp chopped fresh oregano
2.5 ml/½ tsp chopped fresh marjoram
200 g/7 oz can red kidney beans, drained
    and rinsed
15 ml/1 tbsp chopped
    fresh coriander (cilantro)
salt and freshly ground black pepper
chopped fresh marjoram, to garnish
60 ml/4 tbsp sour cream and lettuce leaves,
    to serve

1 Preheat the oven to 220°C/425°F/ Gas 7. Brush or rub the potatoes with a little of the oil and then pierce them with skewers.

2 Place the potatoes on the top shelf of the oven and bake them for about 30 minutes before beginning to cook the chilli.

3 Heat the vegetable oil in a large, heavy pan and add the crushed garlic, chopped onion and red pepper. Fry gently for 4–5 minutes, stirring occasionally, until softened.

4 Add the beef and fry until browned, then stir in the chilli, cumin, cayenne pepper, tomatoes, tomato purée, 60 ml/4 tbsp water and the herbs. Bring to a boil, reduce the heat, then cover and simmer for about 25 minutes, stirring occasionally.

COOK'S TIP: For extra-crispy potatoes, rub with salt after brushing them with the oil in Step 1.

5 Stir in the kidney beans and cook, uncovered, for 5 minutes. Remove from the heat and stir in the chopped coriander. Season well.

6 Cut the baked potatoes in half and place them in warmed serving bowls. Top with the chilli mixture and a dollop of sour cream. Garnish with chopped fresh marjoram and serve hot accompanied by a few lettuce leaves.

Mexican Chilli Beef Tortilla

This is not unlike lasagne, except that the meat is layered between tortillas.

Serves 4

INGREDIENTS
1 onion, chopped
2 garlic cloves, crushed
1 red chilli, seeded and sliced
350 g/12 oz rump steak, cut into small pieces
15 ml/1 tbsp oil
225 g/8 oz/1⅓ cups cooked long grain rice
beef stock, to moisten
3 large wheat tortillas
salt and freshly ground black pepper

FOR THE SALSA PICANTE
2 x 400 g/14 oz cans chopped tomatoes
2 garlic cloves, halved
1 onion, quartered
1–2 red chillies, seeded and roughly chopped
5 ml/1 tsp ground cumin
2.5–5 ml/½–1 tsp cayenne pepper
5 ml/1 tsp chopped fresh oregano tomato
   juice or water, if required

FOR THE CHEESE SAUCE
50 g/2 oz/¼ cup butter
50 g/2 oz/½ cup plain (all-purpose) flour
600 ml/1 pint/2½ cups whole milk
115 g/4 oz/1 cup grated Cheddar cheese

1 Preheat the oven to 180°C/350°F/ Gas 4. To make the salsa picante, place the tomatoes, garlic, onion and chillies in a food processor or blender and process until smooth. Pour into a pan. Add the spices, oregano and salt.

2 Gradually bring to the boil, stirring occasionally. Boil for 1–2 minutes, then lower the heat, cover and simmer for 15 minutes. The sauce should be thick, but of a pouring consistency. If it is too thick, dilute it with a little tomato juice or water.

3 To make the cheese sauce, melt the butter in a pan and stir in the flour. Cook for 1 minute. Add the milk, stirring all the time until the sauce boils and thickens. Stir in all except 30 ml/2 tbsp of the cheese and season to taste. Cover and keep warm.

4 Mix the onion, garlic and chilli in a large bowl. Add the steak and mix well. Heat the oil in a frying pan and stir-fry the meat mixture for about 10 minutes until the meat has browned and the onion is soft. Stir in the rice and enough beef stock to moisten. Season to taste.

5 Pour about a quarter of the cheese sauce into the bottom of a round ovenproof dish. Place a tortilla on top and then spread over half the salsa picante followed by half the meat and rice mixture.

6 Repeat these layers, then add half the remaining cheese sauce and the final tortilla. Pour over the rest of the cheese sauce and sprinkle with the reserved cheese. Bake for 15–20 minutes until golden on top.

Chilli Marinated Beef with Corn-crusted Onion Rings

Fruity, smoky and mild Mexican chillies combine well with garlic in this marinade for grilled steak. Polenta makes a deliciously crunchy coating for the accompanying fried onion rings.

Serves 4

INGREDIENTS
20 g/¾ oz large mild dried red chillies (such as mulato or pasilla)
2 garlic cloves, plain or smoked, finely chopped
5 ml/1 tsp ground toasted cumin seeds
5 ml/1 tsp dried oregano
60 ml/4 tbsp olive oil
4 beef steaks (rump or rib-eye), about 175–225 g/6–8 oz each
salt and freshly ground black pepper

FOR THE ONION RINGS
2 onions, sliced and separated into rings
250 ml/8 fl oz/1 cup milk
75 g/3 oz/½ cup coarse polenta
2.5 ml/½ tsp dried red chilli flakes
5 ml/1 tsp ground toasted cumin seeds
5 ml/1 tsp dried oregano
vegetable oil, for deep-frying

1 Cut the stalks from the chillies and discard the seeds. Toast the chillies in a dry frying pan for 2–4 minutes until they give off their aroma.

2 Place the chillies in a bowl, cover with warm water and leave them to soak for 20–30 minutes.

3 Drain the chillies, reserving the water. Process them with the garlic, toasted cumin seeds, oregano and oil in a food processor or blender to make a thin paste. Add a little of the soaking water, if necessary. Season with freshly ground black pepper.

4 Wash and dry the steaks, rub the chilli marinade all over them and leave to marinate for up to 12 hours.

5 To make the fried onion rings, soak the onions in the milk for 30 minutes.

6 Mix the polenta, dried chilli flakes, ground toasted cumin seeds and oregano in a bowl and season with salt and pepper. Heat the oil for deep-frying to 160–180°C/325–350°F or until a cube of day-old bread browns in about 40–60 seconds.

7 Drain the onion rings and dip them into the polenta mixture to coat them thoroughly. Deep-fry for 2–4 minutes until they are browned and crisp. Do not overcrowd the pan, but cook in batches and keep warm. Drain them on kitchen paper.

8 Heat a barbecue or cast-iron grill pan. Season the steaks with salt and grill for about 4 minutes on each side for a medium result; reduce or increase this time according to how rare or well done you like steak. Serve the steaks with the onion rings.

Chilli Cheese Tortilla with Fresh Tomato Salsa

Green chillies give a Mexican twist to the classic Spanish tortilla recipe, while the tomato salsa adds another chilli kick.

Serves 4

INGREDIENTS
45 ml/3 tbsp sunflower or olive oil
1 small onion, thinly sliced
2–3 jalapeño chillies, seeded and sliced
200 g/7 oz cold cooked potato, thinly sliced
115 g/4 oz/1 cup grated Cheddar cheese
6 eggs, beaten
salt and freshly ground black pepper
Parmesan shavings, to garnish

FOR THE TOMATO SALSA
500 g/1¼ lb tomatoes, skinned, and chopped
1 mild green chilli, seeded and chopped
2 garlic cloves, crushed
45 ml/3 tbsp chopped fresh coriander
   (cilantro)
juice of 1 lime
2.5 ml/½ tsp salt

1 To make the tomato salsa, put the tomatoes in a bowl and add the chopped chilli, garlic, chopped fresh coriander, lime juice and salt. Stir the mixture well and set aside.

2 Heat 15 ml/1 tbsp of the oil in a large frying pan and gently fry the onion and jalapeños for 5 minutes, stirring until softened. Add the potato and cook for 5 minutes until lightly browned, keeping the slices whole.

3 Transfer the cooked vegetables to a warm plate. Wipe the pan with kitchen paper, then add the remaining oil and heat until really hot. Return the vegetables to the pan, scatter the cheese over the top and season.

4 Pour in the beaten eggs, making sure that they seep under the vegetables. Cook over a low heat, without stirring, until the eggs are set.

5 Serve the tortilla cut into wedges, garnished with Parmesan shavings, and with the fresh tomato salsa on the side.

Cheese & Leek Sausages with Tomato, Garlic & Chilli Sauce

These meat-free sausages are based on a Welsh recipe called Glamorgan sausages. The addition of green chilli to the mixture, and the deliciously spicy sauce adds an extra flavour dimension.

Serves 4

INGREDIENTS

25 g/1 oz/2 tbsp butter
175 g/6 oz leeks, finely chopped
1 green chilli, seeded and finely chopped
90 ml/6 tbsp cold mashed potato
115 g/4 oz/2 cups fresh white or wholemeal
    breadcrumbs
150 g/5 oz/1¼ cups grated Caerphilly,
    Lancashire or Cheddar cheese
30 ml/2 tbsp chopped fresh parsley
5 ml/1 tsp chopped fresh sage or marjoram
2 large eggs, beaten
cayenne pepper
65 g/2½ oz/1 cup dry white breadcrumbs
oil, for shallow frying
salt and freshly ground black pepper

FOR THE SAUCE

30 ml/2 tbsp olive oil
2 garlic cloves, thinly sliced
1 red chilli, seeded and finely chopped, or a
    good pinch of dried red chilli flakes
1 small onion, finely chopped
500 g/1¼ lb tomatoes, peeled, seeded
    and chopped
few fresh thyme sprigs
10 ml/2 tsp balsamic or red wine vinegar
pinch of light muscovado sugar
15–30 ml/1–2 tbsp chopped fresh oregano

1 Melt the butter and fry the leeks for 4–5 minutes until softened but not browned. Mix with the chilli, mashed potato, fresh breadcrumbs, cheese, parsley and sage or marjoram. Add sufficient beaten egg (about two-thirds of the quantity) to bind the mixture. Season well with salt and pepper and add a good pinch of cayenne.

2 Shape the mixture into 12 sausage shapes. Dip in the remaining egg, then coat in the dry breadcrumbs. Chill the coated sausages.

3 To make the sauce, heat the oil over a low heat and cook the garlic, chilli and onion for 3–4 minutes. Add the tomatoes, thyme and vinegar. Season with salt, pepper and sugar.

4 Cook the sauce for 40–50 minutes until much reduced. Remove the thyme and purée the sauce in a blender. Reheat with the oregano, then adjust the seasoning to taste, adding more sugar, if necessary.

5 Fry the sausages in shallow oil until they are golden brown on all sides. Drain on kitchen paper and serve with the sauce.

VARIATION: These sausages are also delicious served with garlic mayonnaise or a confit of slow-cooked onions.

Chillies Rellenos

These chillies are filled with a creamy cheese and potato stuffing. Poblanos and Anaheims are quite mild, but you can use hotter chillies if you prefer.

Makes 6

INGREDIENTS
6 poblano or Anaheim chillies
2 potatoes, total weight about 400 g/14 oz, cut into 1 cm/½ in cubes
200 g/7 oz/scant 1 cup cream cheese
200 g/7 oz/1¾ cups grated mature (strong) Cheddar cheese
5 ml/1 tsp salt
2.5 ml/½ tsp freshly ground black pepper
2 eggs, separated
115 g/4 oz/1 cup plain (all-purpose) flour
2.5 ml/½ tsp white pepper
oil, for deep-frying
chilli flakes to garnish (optional)

1 Make a neat slit down one side of each chilli. Place them in a dry frying pan over a moderate heat, turning them frequently until the skin blisters.

2 Place the chillies in a strong plastic bag and tie the top to keep the steam in. Set aside for 20 minutes, then carefully peel off the skin and remove the seeds through the slits, keeping the chillies whole. Dry the chillies with kitchen paper and set them aside.

COOK'S TIP: Take care when making the filling; mix gently, trying not to break up the potato pieces.

3 Cook the potatoes in boiling water for 5 minutes or until just tender. Do not overcook. Drain thoroughly. Put the cream cheese in a bowl and stir in the grated cheese, with 2.5 ml/½ tsp of the salt and the black pepper. Add the potatoes and mix gently.

4 Spoon some of the potato filling into each chilli. Chill for 1 hour so that the filling becomes firm.

5 Whisk the egg whites to firm peaks in a grease-free bowl. In a separate bowl, beat the yolks until pale, then fold in the whites. Scrape on to a large, shallow dish. Spread the flour in another shallow dish and season with the remaining salt and the white pepper.

VARIATION: Whole ancho (dried poblano) chillies can be used instead of fresh chillies, but will need to be reconstituted in water before they can be seeded and stuffed.

6 Heat the oil for deep-frying to 190°C/375°F. Coat a few chillies first in flour and then in egg before adding carefully to the hot oil. Fry in batches until golden and crisp.

7 Drain the chillies on kitchen paper and serve hot, garnished with chilli flakes for extra heat, if desired.

Chilli, Tomato & Spinach Pizza

A richly-flavoured topping with a hint of spice makes this simple and colourful pizza extremely satisfying.

Serves 2

INGREDIENTS
45 ml/3 tbsp tomato oil (from a jar of sun-dried tomatoes)
1 onion, chopped
2 garlic cloves, chopped
1–2 red chillies, seeded and finely chopped
50 g/2 oz (drained weight) sun-dried tomatoes in oil
400 g/14 oz can chopped tomatoes
15 ml/1 tbsp tomato purée (paste)
175 g/6 oz spinach
1 ready-made pizza base, 25–30 cm/10–12 in diameter
75 g/3 oz/¾ cup grated smoked Bavarian cheese, or similar
75 g/3 oz/¾ cup grated mature (strong) Cheddar cheese
salt and freshly ground black pepper

1 Heat 30 ml/2 tbsp of the tomato oil in a pan, add the onion, garlic and chillies and fry them gently for about 5 minutes until they are soft.

2 Roughly chop the sun-dried tomatoes. Add to the pan with the chopped tomatoes, tomato purée and seasoning. Simmer, uncovered, for 15 minutes, stirring occasionally.

3 Remove the tough stalks from the spinach and then wash the leaves in plenty of cold water. Drain them thoroughly and pat them dry with kitchen paper. Roughly chop the spinach leaves.

4 Stir the chopped spinach into the tomato and chilli sauce. Cook the sauce, stirring, for a further 5–10 minutes until the spinach has wilted and no excess moisture remains. Leave the sauce to cool.

5 Meanwhile, preheat the oven to 220°C/425°F/Gas 7. Brush the pizza base with the remaining tomato oil, then spoon the sauce over the top.

6 Sprinkle with the two grated cheeses and bake in the oven for 15–20 minutes until crisp and golden. Serve immediately.

Hot & Sour Chickpeas with Sweet Rice

Chillies provide the heat in this classic hot-sour dish.

Serves 6

INGREDIENTS

350 g/12 oz/1¾ cups dried chickpeas, soaked
    overnight and drained
60 ml/4 tbsp vegetable oil
1 large onion, very finely chopped
225 g/8 oz tomatoes, skinned and
    finely chopped
15 ml/1 tbsp ground coriander
15 ml/1 tbsp ground cumin
5 ml/1 tsp ground fenugreek
5 ml/1 tsp ground cinnamon
1–2 hot green chillies, seeded and finely
    sliced
2.5 cm/1 in piece fresh root ginger, peeled
    and grated
60 ml/4 tbsp lemon juice
15 ml/1 tbsp chopped fresh coriander
    (cilantro)
salt and freshly ground black pepper

FOR THE RICE
40 g/1½ oz/3 tbsp ghee or butter
4 green cardamom pods
4 cloves
350 g/12 oz/1¾ cups basmati rice,
    soaked for 20 minutes and drained
5–10 ml/1–2 tsp granulated sugar
5–6 saffron strands, soaked in warm water

1 Cook the chickpeas in simmering water, covered, for 1–1¼ hours until tender. Drain, reserving the liquid.

2 Heat the oil in a pan. Reserve about 30 ml/2 tbsp of the onion and add the remainder to the pan. Fry for 4–5 minutes, stirring frequently. Add the tomatoes. Cook over a low heat for 5–6 minutes until they are soft.

3 Stir in the ground coriander, cumin, fenugreek and cinnamon. Cook for 30 seconds, then add the chickpeas with 350 ml/12 fl oz/1½ cups of the reserved cooking liquid. Season with salt, cover and simmer gently for 15–20 minutes.

4 Meanwhile, to make the rice, melt the ghee or butter in a pan and fry the cardamom pods and cloves for a few minutes.

5 Remove from the heat and, when the fat has cooled a little, stir in the rice then add 650 ml/22 fl oz/1¼ cups boiling water. Cover tightly and cook for 10 minutes.

6 When the rice is cooked, add the sugar and saffron liquid and stir thoroughly. Cover again. The rice will keep warm while you finish cooking the chickpeas.

7 Mix the reserved onion with the sliced chillies, ginger and lemon juice, and stir into the chickpeas. Add the fresh coriander, adjust the seasoning and serve with the rice.

Lentil Dhal with Chilli & Whole Spices

A tongue-tingling spice mixture is swirled into this purée before serving.

Serves 4–6

INGREDIENTS
40 g/1½ oz/3 tbsp butter or ghee
1 onion, chopped
2 green chillies, seeded and chopped
15 ml/1 tbsp chopped fresh root ginger
225 g/8 oz/1 cup yellow or red lentils
900 ml/1½ pints/3¾ cups water
45 ml/3 tbsp roasted garlic purée (paste)
   (see Cook's Tip)
5 ml/1 tsp ground cumin
5 ml/1 tsp ground coriander
200 g/7 oz tomatoes, peeled and diced
a little lemon juice
salt and freshly ground black pepper
30–45 ml/2–3 tbsp fresh coriander (cilantro)
   leaves, to garnish

FOR THE WHOLE SPICE MIX
30 ml/2 tbsp peanut oil
4–5 shallots, sliced
2 garlic cloves, thinly sliced
15 g/½ oz/1 tbsp butter or ghee
5 ml/1 tsp cumin seeds
5 ml/1 tsp mustard seeds
3–4 small dried red chillies
8–10 fresh curry leaves

1 Melt the butter or ghee in a large pan and cook the chopped onion, chillies and ginger for 10 minutes until golden.

2 Add the lentils and water. Bring to the boil, then part-cover and simmer, stirring occasionally, for 50 minutes or until similar to a very thick soup.

3 Stir in the roasted garlic purée, cumin, ground coriander, salt and pepper. Cook for 10–15 minutes more, uncovered, stirring frequently. Stir in the tomatoes and adjust the seasoning, adding lemon juice to taste.

4 To make the spice mix, heat the oil in a heavy-based pan. Fry the shallots over a medium heat, stirring occasionally, until crisp and browned. Add the garlic and cook, stirring, until it colours slightly. Use a slotted spoon to remove the mixture and keep warm.

COOK'S TIP: For roasted garlic purée, roast garlic cloves at 190°C/375°F/Gas 5 for about 15 minutes until soft, then mash them.

5 Melt the butter or ghee in the same pan. Add the cumin and mustard seeds and fry until the mustard seeds begin to pop. Stir in the dried chillies and curry leaves, then immediately swirl the hot mixture into the cooked dhal. Garnish with the shallot mixture and fresh coriander and serve.

Potatoes with Chillies

If you like chillies, you will simply love these potatoes!

Serves 4

INGREDIENTS
12–14 small new or salad potatoes, halved
30 ml/2 tbsp vegetable oil
2.5 ml/½ tsp crushed dried red chillies
2.5 ml/½ tsp white cumin seeds
2.5 ml/½ tsp fennel seeds
2.5 ml/½ tsp crushed coriander seeds
5 ml/1 tsp salt
1 onion, sliced
1–4 red chillies, chopped
15 ml/1 tbsp chopped fresh coriander
  (cilantro), plus extra to garnish

1 Cook the potatoes in boiling salted water until tender but still firm. Drain thoroughly and set aside.

2 In a deep frying pan, heat the vegetable oil over a medium heat. Add the crushed dried chillies, cumin, fennel and coriander seeds and salt and fry, stirring continuously, for 30–40 seconds to release their aroma.

3 Add the sliced onion and fry for about 10 minutes, until golden brown. Add the cooked potatoes, chopped red chillies and fresh coriander and stir well.

4 Reduce the heat to very low, then cover and cook for 5–7 minutes. Serve the potatoes hot, garnished with more fresh coriander.

Red Chilli Cauliflower

The cauliflower here is flavoured with a spicy tomato salsa and fresh cheese.

Serves 6

INGREDIENTS
1 small onion, very finely chopped
grated rind and juice of 1 lime
400 g/14 oz can chopped tomatoes
4 serrano chillies, seeded and finely chopped
1.5 ml/¼ tsp caster (superfine) sugar
1 medium cauliflower, divided into florets
75 g/3 oz/¾ cup crumbled feta cheese
salt
chopped fresh flat leaf parsley, to garnish

1 In a bowl, mix the onion with the lime rind and juice. Set aside so that the lime juice can soften the onion.

2 Tip the tomatoes into a pan and add the chillies and sugar. Heat gently. Meanwhile, cook the cauliflower in boiling water for 5–8 minutes, until tender, then drain.

3 Add the onion mixture to the tomatoes with salt to taste, stir and heat through, then spoon about one-third of the salsa into a serving dish.

4 Arrange the cauliflower on top of the salsa and spoon the remaining salsa on top. Sprinkle with the feta, which should soften a little on contact. Serve immediately, sprinkled with parsley.

Mushrooms with Chipotle Chillies

The smoky flavour of chipotles is the perfect foil for mushrooms.

Serves 6

INGREDIENTS
2 chipotle chillies
450 g/1 lb/6 cups button (white) mushrooms
60 ml/4 tbsp vegetable oil
1 onion, finely chopped
2 garlic cloves, crushed or chopped
salt
small bunch of fresh coriander (cilantro), to
  garnish

1 Soak the dried chillies in a bowl of hot water for about 10 minutes. Drain, cut off the stalks, then slit the chillies scrape out the seeds, and chop finely.

2 Trim the button mushrooms, then clean them with a damp cloth or kitchen paper. If they are large, cut them in half.

3 Heat the oil in a large frying pan. Add the onion, garlic, chillies and mushrooms and stir until evenly coated in the oil. Fry for 6–8 minutes, stirring occasionally, until the onion and mushrooms are tender.

4 Season to taste and spoon into a serving dish. Chop some of the coriander, leaving some leaves whole, and use as a garnish. Serve hot.

Chilli Vegetables in Coconut Milk

A delicious Thai way of cooking vegetables with plenty of chillies.

Serves 4–6

INGREDIENTS

450 g/1 lb mixed vegetables, such as aubergines (eggplants), baby sweetcorn, carrots, asparagus and patty pan squash
8 red chillies, seeded
2 lemon grass stalks, chopped
4 kaffir lime leaves, torn
30 ml/2 tbsp vegetable oil
250 ml/8 fl oz/1 cup coconut milk
30 ml/2 tbsp Thai fish sauce
salt
15–20 Thai basil leaves and 1 fresh red chilli, thinly sliced, to garnish

1 Cut the vegetables into similar-size pieces using a sharp knife. Put the chillies, lemon grass and kaffir lime leaves in a mortar and grind together with a pestle.

2 Heat the oil in a wok or large, deep frying pan. Add the chilli mixture and fry for 2–3 minutes. Stir in the coconut milk and bring to the boil.

3 Add the vegetables and cook for about 5 minutes or until they are tender. Season with the fish sauce and salt and garnish with basil and chilli.

Roasted Pepper Salad

Dried chilli flakes give an extra lift to this colourful salad.

Serves 4

INGREDIENTS
3 red (bell) peppers
6 large plum tomatoes
2.5 ml/½ tsp dried red chilli flakes
1 red onion, finely sliced
3 garlic cloves, finely chopped
grated rind and juice of 1 lemon
45 ml/3 tbsp chopped fresh flat leaf parsley
30 ml/2 tbsp extra virgin olive oil
salt and freshly ground black pepper
black and green olives and extra chopped
    fresh flat leaf parsley, to garnish

1 Preheat the oven to 220°C/425°F/
Gas 7. Place the peppers on a baking
sheet and roast, turning occasionally,
for 10 minutes or until the skins are
almost blackened.

2 Add the tomatoes to the baking
sheet and bake for 5 minutes more.

3 Place the peppers in a strong plastic
bag, close the top, trapping in the
steam, and set aside, with the tomatoes,
until they are cool enough to handle.

4 Carefully pull the skin off the
peppers. Remove the seeds, then chop
the peppers and tomatoes roughly and
place in a mixing bowl.

5 Add the chilli flakes, onion, garlic,
lemon rind and juice. Sprinkle over
the parsley. Mix well, then transfer to a
serving dish. Season to taste, drizzle
over the olive oil and scatter olives and
extra parsley over the top. Serve at
room temperature.

Spinach Salad with Chilli

Serrano chillies are the "secret weapon" hidden in these spinach leaves.

Serves 6

INGREDIENTS
500 g/1¼ lb baby spinach leaves
50 g/2 oz/⅓ cup sesame seeds
50 g/2 oz/¼ cup butter
30 ml/2 tbsp olive oil
6 shallots, sliced
9 serrano chillies, seeded and cut into strips
4 tomatoes, sliced

FOR THE DRESSING
6 roasted garlic cloves (see page 56)
120 ml/4 fl oz/½ cup white wine vinegar
2.5 ml/½ tsp ground white pepper
1 bay leaf
2.5 ml/½ tsp ground allspice
30 ml/2 tbsp chopped fresh thyme, plus a
  few whole sprigs to garnish

1 To make the dressing, remove the skins from the garlic when cool, then chop and combine with the remaining ingredients in a screw-top jar. Chill.

2 Wash and dry the spinach. Toast the sesame seeds in a dry frying pan, shaking frequently over a moderate heat until golden. Set aside.

3 Heat the butter and oil in a frying pan. Fry the shallots for 4–5 minutes until softened, then stir in most of the chilli strips and fry for 2–3 minutes more. In a bowl, layer the spinach with the shallot mixture, and the tomato slices. Pour over the dressing. Sprinkle with sesame seeds and serve, garnished with thyme sprigs and chilli strips.

Index

Avocado, chilli & red onion salsa, 15

Barbecued jerk chicken, 34

Caribbean chilli-spiced fish cakes with tomato dip, 28
Cheese & leek sausages with tomato, garlic & chilli sauce, 48
Chicken with chipotle sauce, 32
Chilli cheese tortilla with fresh tomato salsa, 46
Chilli crabs, 27
Chilli marinated beef with corn-crusted onion rings, 44
Chilli onion koftas, 20

Chilli vegetables in coconut milk, 61
Chilli, tomato & basil dip, 14
Chilli, tomato & spinach pizza, 52
Chillies rellenos, 50
Corn & sweet potato soup with chilli, 10

Fiery fish & shellfish, 22

Hot & sour chickpeas with sweet rice, 54
Hot & sour soup, 12
Hot chilli chicken 35
Hot Vegetarian dishes, 46

Indian-spiced fish stew, 26

Lentil dhal with chilli &

whole spices, 56

Marinated squid risotto with chilli, 30
Mexican chilli beef tortilla, 42
Mushrooms with chipotle chillis, 60
Mussels with a chilli sauce, 17

Penne with tomato & chilli sauce, 36
Piquant side dishes & salads, 58
Piri-piri prawns with aïoli, 16
Potatoes with chillies, 58

Red chilli cauliflower, 59

Red snapper with chilli, gin & ginger sauce, 24
Roasted pepper salad, 62

Sizzling Chicken & meat dishes, 32
Spicy chicken soup, 12
Spicy lamb & potato curry, 38
Spicy potato wedges with chilli dip, 18
Spicy soups, dips & appetizers, 10
Spinach salad with chilli, 63
Steamed fish with red chilli sauce, 22

Tex-mex baked potatoes with chilli, 40
Types of chilli, 6–7

This edition is published by Lorenz Books, an imprint of Anness Publishing Ltd, 108 Great Russell Street, London WC1B 3NA info@anness.com www.annesspublishing.com; twitter: @Anness_Books

© Anness Publishing Limited 2015

If you like the images in this book and would like to investigate using them for publishing, promotions or advertising, please visit our website www.practicalpictures.com for more information.

Publisher: Joanna Lorenz
Editor: Valerie Ferguson & Helen Sudell
Production Controller: Pirong Wang

Recipes contributed by: Angela Boggiano, Kit Chan, Silvano Franco, Shirley Gill, Brian Glover, Rosamund Grant, Christine Ingram, Manisha Kanani, Lesley Mackley, Sally Mansfield, Norma Miller, Jane Milton, Sallie Morris, Jeni Wright.

Photography: William Adams-Lingwood, Karl Adamson, Janine Hosegood, David Jordan, Dave King, Patrick McLeavey, Steve Moss, Thomas Odulate, Simon Smith, Sam Stowell.

A CIP catalogue record for this book is available from the British Library

COOK'S NOTES

Bracketed terms are intended for American readers.

For all recipes, quantities are given in both metric and imperial measures and, where appropriate, in standard cups and spoons. Follow one set of measures, but not a mixture.

Standard spoon and cup measures are level. 1 tsp = 5ml, 1 tbsp = 15ml, 1 cup = 250ml/8fl oz. Australian standard tablespoons are 20ml. Australian readers should use 3 tsp in place of 1 tbsp for measuring small quantities.

American pints are 16fl oz/2 cups. American readers should use 20fl oz/2.5 cups in place of 1 pint when measuring liquids.

Electric oven temperatures in this book are for conventional ovens. When using a fan oven, the temperature will probably need to be reduced by about 10–20°C/20–40°F. Check with your manufacturer's instruction book for guidance.

Medium (US large) eggs are used unless otherwise stated.